TRIGGER - VOL I

100 FILM RECOMMENDATIONS

SUURESH RAMACHANDRAN

For Mama and Papa

Foreword
Each of these Films is a Film I have seen and liked.
Sure, we have personal preferences. Some of us like a film, others do not.
But tell me any of these Films is 'not well made' and I'll change my line.
Obviously these are not Films everyone has heard of. Well-known Films do not need a book like this.
Even though the Descriptors are quite brief, it was a challenge to write them.
I have tried to tickle your curiosity and indicate the genre, without giving any of the story away.
Why 'Trigger'? Trigger suggests Action Films which most of us love. More importantly, it suggests triggering the imagination.
I'm sure this book will serve as guide, reference and record, even to me.
Take Shelter
Cast: Michael Shannon, Jessica Chastain, Tova Stewart, Shea Whigham

Director: Jeff Nichols

Year released: 2011

Description:
One person in a remote seaside village is imagining that a storm is going to come anytime. What's interesting is, how an air of impending doom has been created throughout the Film.

Come next spring
Cast: Ann Sheridan and Steve Cochran

Director: R.G. Springsteen

Year released: 1956

Description: A beautiful story about love, forgiveness and family

Sidekicks
Cast: Jonathan Brandis, Chuck Norris.

Director: Aaron Norris

Year released: 1992

Description: An asthmatic boy dreams of becoming an action star like
Chuck Norris.

The StrangerCast: Edward G. Robinson, Loretta Young, and Orson
Welles

Director: Orson Welles
Year released: 1946

Description: A war crimes investigator tracks a high-ranking Nazi
fugitive

All My Sons
Cast: Edward G. Robinson and Burt Lancaster.

Director: Irving Reis

Year released: 1948

Description:

A manufacturer of aircraft cylinders finally realises his folly in dispatching parts he knew were faulty.

16 wishesCast: Debby Ryan and Jean-Luc Bilodeau

Director: Peter DeLuise

Year released: 2010

Description: A young girl makes 16 wishes before her 16th birthday. Then what happens?

My Boss's DaughterCast: Ashton Kutcher, Tara Reid and Terence Stamp

Director: David Zucker

Year released: 2003

Description: A man is asked to housesit for his boss. He tries to take the opportunity to get closer to the boss's daughter. Will the journey be a cakewalk?

Letters to JulietCast: Amanda Seyfried, Christopher Egan, Gael García Bernal, Vanessa Redgrave and Franco Nero

Director: Gary Winick
Year released: 2010

Description:
An elderly couple finds long-lost love in the backdrop of a trip to Verona.

Diplomatic CourierCast: Tyrone Power, Patricia Neal and Stephen McNally

Director: Henry Hathaway

Year released: 1952

Description: Espionage, sabotage, spies and thrill.

The Trouble With HarryCast: Edmund Gwenn, John Forsythe, Mildred Natwick, Jerry Mathers and Shirley MacLaine

Director: Alfred Hitchcock

Year released: 1955

Description: A dead body appears in a small house in a village. What happens next?

IndiscreetCast: Cary Grant and Ingrid Bergman.

Director: Stanley Done

Year released: 1958

Description: A beautiful woman falls in love with a married man

Judgement in BerlinCast: Martin Sheen, Sam Wanamaker and Sean Penn

Director: Leo Penn

Year released: 1988

Description: An American judge in Germany faces a tough decision
Perfect WitnessCast: Brian Dennehy, Aidan Quinn, Stockard Channing, Laura Harrington, Delroy Lindo and Joe Grifas

Director: Robert Mandel

Year released: 1989

Description:
The owner of a small restaurant becomes the witness to a gangland killing, Will he testify in court?

MistrialCast: Bill Pullman, Jon Seda, and Robert Loggia

Director: Heywood Gould

Year released: 1996

Description: A cop takes out his gun in the middle of the court.
Where will the Film go from here?

Too Many Husbands
Cast: Jean Arthur, Fred MacMurray and Melvyn Dougla

Director: Wesley Ruggles

Year released: 1940

Description:
An ex-lover presumed dead returns while the girl has found a new
love.

Undercover Angel
Cast: Yasmine Bleeth and Dean Winters.

Director: Bryan Michael Stoller

Year released: 1999

Description: A struggling writer's life is turned around by a little girl

Suddenly
Cast: Frank Sinatra and Sterling Hayden, James Gleason and Nancy
Gates.

Director: Lewis Allen

Year released: 1954

Description:
A group of assassins take a family hostage with the intent to shoot the President.

The Card
Cast: Alec Guinness, Glynis Johns, Valerie Hobson, Petula Clark

Director: Ronald Neame

Year released: 1952

Description: A young man of poor circumstances wishes to rise in the world.

The Million Pound Note
Cast: Gregory Peck

Director: Ronald Neame

Year released: 1954

Description: Two aristocrats give a young man a loan without telling him it's a single million pound note.

Lethal Vows
Cast: John Ritter, Marg Helgenberger and Megan Gallagher, t

Director: Paul Schneider

Year released: 1999

Description: An ailing woman realises that her husband might be deliberately poisoning her. Based on a true story.

The Pilot's Wife
Cast: Christine Lahti, Campbell Scott, and John Heard

Director: Robert Markowitz

Year released: 2002

Description:A pilot's wife discovers after he dies in a crash, that he was associated with the IRA and there was another woman in his life.

Sleuth
Cast: Laurence Olivier and Michael Caine

Director: Joseph L. Mankiewicz

Year released: 1972

Description: This is a 2 hr 20 min Film with two actors. Two actors only. Need to know more?

Secret Agent
Cast: Madeleine Carroll, Peter Lorre, John Gielgud, and Robert Young

Director: Alfred Hitchcock

Year released: 1936
Description: A WW I spy and espionage story

Prudence and the Pill
Cast: Deborah Kerr and David Niven with Robert Coote, Irina Demick, Joyce Redman, Judy Geeson, Keith Michell, Michael Hordern and Edith Evans.

Director: Fielder Cook and Ronald Neame

Year released: 1963

Description: Five couples attempt to avoid pregnancy by using contraceptive pills

Infidelity in Suburbia
Cast: Sarah Butler, Marcus Rosner, Peter Benson, Arlo Hajdu

Director: David Winning

Year released: 2017

Description: A tale about infidelity, as the title explains.

By Appointment Only
Cast: Ally Walker

Director: John Terlesky

Year released: 2007

Description: A mysterious man enters the life of a real estate agent and her son.

A Frosty Affair
Cast: Jewel Staite, Shawn Roberts, Cindy Busby

Director: Dylan Pearce

Year released: 2015

Description: A teacher, travelling to the city for her marriage, is forced by circumstances to travel with a stranger. What happens next?

Pocketful of Miracles
Cast: Bette Davis and Glenn Ford

Director: Frank Capra

Year released: 1961

Description: Glenn Ford, Bette Davis and Frank Capra. I'd give this Film 7 stars if I could.

Sunday in New York
Cast: Jane Fonda, Rod Taylor and Cliff Robertson.

Director: Peter Tewksbury

Year released: 1963

Description: This is a romantic comedy with several twists and turns.

Revenge of the Bridesmaids
Cast: Raven-Symoné and Joanna García

Director: James Hayman

Year released: 2010

Description: How two bridesmaids foil a sham wedding to reunite old lovers

A Strange Affair
Cast: Judith Light and Jay Thomas.

Director: Ted Kotcheff

Year released: 1996

Description: A love triangle need not go one way or the other. Nail-biting suspense

The Fixer
Cast: Jon Voight, Brenda Bakke, J.J. Johnston

Director: Charles Robert Carner

Year released: 1998

Description: A lawyer with no scruples of conscience is finally forced to face some hard truths

Flight
Cast: Denzel Washington

Director: Robert Zemeckis

Year released: 2012

Description: An airline pilot crashlands his plane. Everyone survives but it is later revealed that he was flying under the influence of alcohol and cocaine.

Mr Deeds goes to town
Cast: Gary Cooper and Jean Arthur

Director: Frank Capra

Year released: 1936

Description: A small town poet inherits 20 million dollars from his uncle. For obvious reasons, drama follows.

Underground
Cast: Jeffrey Lynn and Philip Dorn

Director: Vincent Sherman

Year released: 1941

Description: Two brothers on opposite sides of the political spectrum. One, a Nazi and the other, part of the German Nazi resistance.

Fools Parade
Cast: James Stewart and George Kennedy

Director: Andrew V. McLaglen

Year released: 1971

Description: Sometimes criminals and lawkeepers play opposing roles.
The Ratings Game
Cast: Danny DeVito and Rhea Perlman,

Director: Danny DeVito

Year released: 1984

Description:
This is a comedy film that will make you cry. The title gives you an
idea of the subject - TV Ratings.
Boychoir (also known as 'Hear my Song')

Cast: Dustin Hoffman, Kathy Bates, Debra Winger, Josh Lucas

Director: François Girard
Year released: 2015
Description: What happens to an illegitimate child

Never been kissed
Cast: Drew Barrymore, Jessica Alba, David Arquette, Michael Vartan,

Director: Raja Gosnell

Year released: 1999

Description: A beautiful, simple girl getting on in years finally finds love.

The Fifth Mind
Cast: Julia Duvall, Jack Diamond, Victoria Gilson,

Director: Naoko Tajima

Year released: 2007

Description: Two siblings with a shared traumatic childhood experience find different ways to deal with it.

Soldier Boy
Cast: Andrey Andreev, Darya Ursulyak, Viktor Dobronravov

Director: Viktoria Fanasiutina

Year released: 2019

Description: A young boy loses his parents to war and is adopted by a German regiment. A true story.

Murder by Contract
Cast: Vince Edwards

Director: Irving Lerner

Year released: 1958

Description: Martin Scorsese, cited Murder by Contract as "the film that has influenced [him] most." (Wikipedia)

The Big Combo
Cast: Cornel Wilde, Richard Conte and Brian Donlev

Director: Joseph H. Lewis
Year released: 1955

Description: A cop and criminal story

The Bravados
Cast: Gregory Peck and Joan Collins

Director: Henry King

Year released: 1958

Description: A western. A rancher pursues 4 outlaws he thought killed his wife.

Winter of Frozen Dreams
Cast: Thora Birch, Keith Carradine, and Brendan Sexton II

Director: Eric Mandelbaum

Year released: 2009

Description: A detective pursues a complex female killer.

I'll be seeing you
Cast: Alison Eastwood, Iris Quinn, Bo Swenson

Director: Will Dixon

Year released: 2004
Description: A young woman discovers truths about her father.

Good Day for it
Cast: Robert Patrick, Samantha Mathis, Lance Henriksen

Director: Nick Stagliano

Year released: 2011

Description: Family, crime and revenge

Istanbul
Cast: Errol Flynn, Cornell Borchers

Director: Joseph Pevney

Year released: 1957

Description: Decidedly a thriller with a liberal dose of romance

The Walking Target
Cast: Joan Evans, Merry Anders, and Ronald Foster.

Director: Edward L. Cahn

Year released: 1960

Description: The story follows an ex-convict.

The Inspectors
Cast: Louis Gossett Jr., Jonathan Silverman, Tobias Mehler

Director: Brad Turner

Year released: 1998

Description: The Inspectors here are not cops, but Postal Inspectors, and who says there's any less thrill in the lives of Postal Inspectors.

Broken Trust
Cast: Tom Selleck, Elizabeth McGovern, William Atherton
Director: Geoffrey Sax

Year released: 1995

Description: Corruption in the courtroom

Patterns
Cast: Van Heflin, Everett Sloane, and Ed Begley

Director: Fielder Cook

Year released: 1956

Description: Niceness vs Toughness in a corporate context

Behind the Mask
Cast: Donald Sutherland, Mathew Fox, Mary McDonnell

Director: Tom McLoughlin

Year released: 1999
Description: A relationship story. I have the highest respect for Donald Sutherland.

Steel Toes
Cast: David Strathairn

Director: David Gow, Mark Adam

Year released: 2007

Description: A lawyer faces the toughest challenge of his life.

What's Eating Gilbert Grape
Cast: Johnny Depp, Leonardo DiCaprio, Juliette Lewis and Darlene Cates

Director: Lasse Hallström

Year released: 1993
Description: Shot when Leonardo Dicaprio was barely 19. You'll discover why he is such a phenomenal talent.

Night Alarm
Cast: Bruce Cabot

Director: Spencer Gordon Bennet
Year released: 1934

Description: A reporter seeks some excitement

A Strange Adventure
Cast: Joan Evans, Ben Cooper, Marla English, Jan Merlin, Nick Adams
and Peter Miller.

Director: William Witney

Year released: 1956

Description: A thriller, a 3-ller, actually.

Half a sinner
Cast: Heather Angel

Director: Al Christie

Year released: 1940

Description: A young schoolteacher seeks adventure.
Undercover Agent
Cast: Russell Gleason, Shirley Deane, and J. M. Kerrigan

Director: Howard Bretherton

Year released: 1939

Description: The undercover agent is a railway postal clerk

Heat
Cast: Al Pacino, Robert De Niro, Tom Sizemore, Jon Voight, Val Kilmer

Director: Michael Mann

Year released: 1995

Description: Cops and criminals and relationships

They made me a fugitive
Cast: Trevor Howard, Sally Gray

Director: Alberto Cavalcanti

Year released: 1947

Description: A law-abiding citizen falls into the grip of crime, as the title indicates.

Kiss and Tell
Cast: Cheryl Ladd, John Terry and Francie Swift

Director: Andy Wolk

Year released: 1996

Description: A wife's dream life is disturbed by her husband's probable mistress.

So Goes my Love
Cast: Myrna Loy, Don Ameche

Director: Frank Ryan

Year released: 1946

Description: A relationship film with humour. Based on a true story.

Blue, White and Perfect
Cast: Lloyd Nolan, Mary Beth Hughes, and Helene Reynolds

Director: Herbert I. Leeds

Year released: 1942

Description: An American private detective mystery film

Somewhere in the night

Cast: John Hodiak and Nancy Guild

Director: Joseph L. Mankiewicz

Year released: 1946

Description: An amnesiac American soldier returns from World War II badly injured. He tries to find his old identity and stumbles on a murder mystery.

The Contract
· Cast: Morgan Freeman, John Cusack

Director: Bruce Beresford
Year released: 2006

Description: The paths of a contract killer and an ordinary schoolteacher cross.
Exemplary Officer
Korean Film
Description:
A man is accused by his wife of being 'a very boring person' and that

very day turns out to be the most exciting day in his life.
For all time
Cast: Mark Harmon, Mary McDonnell, and Catherine Hicks

Director: Steven Schachter
Year released: 2000

Description: A beautiful story around time travel

Across the bridge
Cast: Rod Steiger and Bernard Lee

Director: Ken Annakin

Year released: 1957

Description: This Film will surprise you and could make you cry

The Take
Cast: Billy Dee Williams, Eddie Albert, Frankie Avalon, Sorrell Booke, Tracy Reed, and Albert Salmi.

Director: Robert Hartford-Davis

Year released: 1974

Description: As the title suggests, this is the story of a cop 'on the take'.
It's a wonderful world
Cast: Claudette Colbert and James Stewart

Director: W. S. Van Dyke

Year released: 1939

Description: Suspense, action, thrill, romance, comedy, the film inhabits a wonderful world.

State of the Union
· Cast: Spencer Tracy, Katharine Hepburn, Van Johnson

Director: Frank Capra

Year released: 2005

Description: Drama around a man running for President. Wit of the highest order.

A farewell to arms
Cast: Rock Hudson, Jennifer Jones, Vittorio De Sica

Director: Charles Vidor, John Huston

Year released: 1957

Description: Romance in the backdrop of World War I

Behind Green Lights
Cast: Carole Landis, William Gargan, Don Beddoe

Director: Otto Brower

Year released: 1946

Description: A story with cops, criminals, journalists and politicians

Account Rendered
Cast: Griffith Jones, Ursula Howells and Honor Blackman

Director: Peter Graham Scott

Year released: 1957

Description: A crime film

Fear No More
Cast: Mala Powers, Jacques Bergerac and Anna Lee Carroll.

Director: Bernard Wiesen

Year released: 1961

Description: A woman becomes a murder suspect

Escape in the fog
Cast: Otto Kruger, Nina Foch and William Wright

Director: Budd Boetticher
Year released: 1945

Description: A woman's premonition in the backdrop of war, spies and crime

Tokyo File 212
Cast: Florence Marly, Robert Peyton, Tetsu Nakamura

Director: Dorrell McGowan, Stuart E. McGowan

Year released: 1951

Description: A Japanese-American co-production of a spy film.

Identity Unknown
Cast: Richard Arlen, Cheryl Walker, Roger Pryor

Director: Walter Colmes

Year released: 1945

Description: Near the end of World War II, an amnesiac soldier must find his true identity.

Point Last Seen
Cast: Linda Hamilton, Kevin Kilner, Sam Hennings

Director: Elodie Keene

Year released: 1998

Description: A tracker searches for a little girl in the desert, and confronts the pain of her own loss.

Cause for Alarm

Cast: Loretta Young, Barry Sullivan, Bruce Cowling

Director: Tay Garnett

Year released: 1951

Description: A suspense film revolving around a letter

Never Let go
Cast: Richard Todd, Peter Sellers and Elizabeth Sellars

Director: John Guillermin

Year released: 1960

Description: A petty car thief steals a particular car and drama
unfolds

Jack and Sarah
Cast: Richard E. Grant, Samantha Mathis, Judi Dench, Eileen Atkins,
Cherie Lunghi, Ian McKellen

Director: Tim Sullivan

Year released: 1995

Description: Fathers and daughters. And daughters and fathers.

The Outsider
Cast: Tim Daly and Naomi Watts

Director: Randa Haines

Year released: 2002

Description: A western with romance.

The Girl in the Cafe
Cast: Bill Nighy, Kelly Macdonald, Marit Velle Kile

Director: David Yates

Year released: 2005

Description: What happens when a top bureaucrat asks a simply girl
to accompany him to a high-profile event

That Uncertain feeling
Cast: Merle Oberon, Melvyn Douglas and Burgess Meredith

Director: Ernst Lubitsch
Year released: 1941

Description: A lovely comedy with romance.

Guest in the House
Cast: Anne Baxter and Ralph Bellamy

Director: John Brahm

Year released: 1944

Description: A cranky, conspiring woman throws a family into disarray

The Third Visitor
Cast: Sonia Dresdel, Guy Middleton and Karel Stepanek

Director: Maurice Elvey

Year released: 1951

Description: Have you seen a thriller where the suspense is maintained almost till the last frame?

The House of Mystery
· Cast: Ed Lowry, Verna Hillie, John Sheehan

Director: William Nigh

Year released: 1934

Description: An ancient curse and a killer ape

The Ghost Train
Cast: : Arthur Askey; Richard Murdoch

Director: Walter Forde

Year released: 1941

Description: Some train passengers are stranded in the night and drama follows

I killed that man
Cast: Ricardo Cortez, Ralf Harolde

Director: Phil Rosen

Year released: 1941

Description: How the mastermind is revealed

Emergency Wedding
Cast: Larry Parks, Barbara Hale.

Director: Edward Buzzell

Year released: 1950

Description: How a rich brat comes to his senses

In the French Style
Cast: Jean Seberg, Stanley Baker and Philippe Forquet

Director: Robert Parrish

Year released: 1963

Description: A young girl's discovery of life in the backdrop of art

Phone call from a stranger
Cast: Gary Merrill, Bette Davis, Shelley Winters, Michael Rennie, Keenan Wynn

Director: Jean Negulesco

Year released: 1952

Description: When you reach about 60% of the Film, you will learn why this is such an apt title for this Film.

The Lineup
Cast: Eli Wallach, Robert Keith, Warner Anderson

Director: Don Siegel

Year released: 1958

Description: Two cops and drugdealers

The Trollenberg terror
Cast: Forrest Tucker, Laurence Payne, Jennifer Jayne and Janet Munro.

Director: Quentin Lawrence

Year released: 1958

Description: An early special effects Film with extra-terrrestrials
Deadly whispers

Cast: Tony Danza, Pamela Reed

Director: Bill L. Norton

Year released: 1995

Description: A man's mental disorder is the centrepiece of this murder mystery

A closed book
Cast: Daryl Hannah, Jane Ryder, Tom Conti

Director: Raúl Ruiz

Year released: 2010

Description: A blind author and his secretary promise riveting drama

Against a crooked sky
Cast: Richard Boone, Stewart Petersen, Henry Wilcoxon.

Director: Earl Bellamy

Year released: 1975

Description: This is a western with a relatively large landscape, literally and figuratively

A lady takes a chance
Cast: Jean Arthur and John Wayne

Director: William A. Seiter

Year released: 1943

Description: Three guys are behind a girl when she meets a fourth

Contents

Contents

Contents

Contents

Contents

Foreword

Each of these Films is a Film I have seen and liked.

Sure, we have personal preferences. Some of us like a film, others do not.

But tell me any of these Films is 'not well made' and I'll change my line.

Obviously these are not Films everyone has heard of. Well-known Films do not need a book like this.

Even though the Descriptors are quite brief, it was a challenge to write them.

I have tried to tickle your curiosity and indicate the genre, without giving any of the story away.

Why 'Trigger'? Trigger suggests Action Films which most of us love.

More importantly, it suggests triggering the imagination.

I'm sure this book will serve as guide, reference and record, even to me.

Acknowledgements

Deepest gratitude to the Universe

Take Shelter

Cast: Michael Shannon, Jessica Chastain, Tova Stewart, Shea Whigham

Director: Jeff Nichols

Year released: 2011

Description:

One person in a remote seaside village is imagining that a storm is going to come anytime. What's interesting is, how an air of impending doom has been created throughout the Film.

Come next spring

Cast: Ann Sheridan and Steve Cochran
Director: R.G. Springsteen
Year released: 1956
Description: A beautiful story about love, forgiveness and family

Sidekicks

Cast: Jonathan Brandis, Chuck Norris.
Director: Aaron Norris
Year released: 1992
Description: An asthmatic boy dreams of becoming an action star like Chuck Norris.

The Stranger

Cast: Edward G. Robinson, Loretta Young, and Orson Welles

Director: Orson Welles

Year released: 1946

Description: A war crimes investigator tracks a high-ranking Nazi fugitive

All My Sons

Cast: Edward G. Robinson and Burt Lancaster.
Director: Irving Reis
Year released: 1948
Description:
A manufacturer of aircraft cylinders finally realises his folly in dispatching parts he knew were faulty.

16 wishes

Cast: Debby Ryan and Jean-Luc Bilodeau
    Director: Peter DeLuise
    Year released: 2010
    Description: A young girl makes 16 wishes before her 16th birthday. Then what happens?

My Boss's Daughter

Cast: Ashton Kutcher, Tara Reid and Terence Stamp
Director: David Zucker
Year released: 2003
Description: A man is asked to housesit for his boss. He tries to take the opportunity to get closer to the boss's daughter. Will the journey be a cakewalk?

Letters to Juliet

Cast: Amanda Seyfried, Christopher Egan, Gael García Bernal, Vanessa Redgrave and Franco Nero

Director: Gary Winick

Year released: 2010

Description:

An elderly couple finds long-lost love in the backdrop of a trip to Verona.

Diplomatic Courier

Cast: Tyrone Power, Patricia Neal and Stephen McNally
Director: Henry Hathaway
Year released: 1952
Description: Espionage, sabotage, spies and thrill.

The Trouble With Harry

Cast: Edmund Gwenn, John Forsythe, Mildred Natwick, Jerry Mathers and Shirley MacLaine

Director: Alfred Hitchcock

Year released: 1955

Description: A dead body appears in a small house in a village. What happens next?

Indiscreet

Cast: Cary Grant and Ingrid Bergman.
Director: Stanley Done
Year released: 1958
Description: A beautiful woman falls in love with a married man

Judgement in Berlin

Cast: Martin Sheen, Sam Wanamaker and Sean Penn
Director: Leo Penn
Year released: 1988
Description: An American judge in Germany faces a tough decision

Perfect Witness

Cast: Brian Dennehy, Aidan Quinn, Stockard Channing, Laura Harrington, Delroy Lindo and Joe Grifas
   Director: Robert Mandel
   Year released: 1989
   Description:
   The owner of a small restaurant becomes the witness to a gangland killing, Will he testify in court?

Mistrial

Cast: Bill Pullman, Jon Seda, and Robert Loggia
  Director: Heywood Gould
  Year released: 1996
  Description: A cop takes out his gun in the middle of the court. Where will the Film go from here?

Too Many Husbands

Cast: Jean Arthur, Fred MacMurray and Melvyn Douglas
Director: Wesley Ruggles
Year released: 1940
Description:
An ex-lover presumed dead returns while the girl has found a new love.

Undercover Angel

Cast: Yasmine Bleeth and Dean Winters.
   Director: Bryan Michael Stoller
   Year released: 1999
   Description: A struggling writer's life is turned around by a little girl

Suddenly

Cast: Frank Sinatra and Sterling Hayden, James Gleason and Nancy Gates.

Director: Lewis Allen

Year released: 1954

Description: A group of assassins take a family hostage with the intent to shoot the President.

The Card

Cast: Alec Guinness, Glynis Johns, Valerie Hobson, Petula Clark

Director: Ronald Neame

Year released: 1952

Description: A young man of poor circumstances wishes to rise in the world.

The Million Pound Note

Cast: Gregory Peck
   Director: Ronald Neame
   Year released: 1954
   Description: Two aristocrats give a young man a loan without telling him it's a single million pound note.

Lethal Vows

Cast: John Ritter, Marg Helgenberger, Megan Gallagher
Director: Paul Schneider
Year released: 1999
Description: An ailing woman realises that her husband might be deliberately poisoning her. Based on a true story.

The Pilot's Wife

Cast: Christine Lahti, Campbell Scott, and John Heard
Director: Robert Markowitz
Year released: 2002
Description:A pilot's wife discovers after he dies in a crash, that he was associated with the IRA and there was another woman in his life.

Sleuth

Cast: Laurence Olivier and Michael Caine
  Director: Joseph L. Mankiewicz
  Year released: 1972
  Description: This is a 2 hr 20 min Film with two actors.
Two actors only. Need to know more?

Secret Agent

Cast: Madeleine Carroll, Peter Lorre, John Gielgud, and Robert Young

Director: Alfred Hitchcock

Year released: 1936

Description: A WW I spy and espionage story

Prudence and the Pill

Cast: Deborah Kerr and David Niven with Robert Coote, Irina Demick, Joyce Redman, Judy Geeson, Keith Michell, Michael Hordern and Edith Evans.

Director: Fielder Cook and Ronald Neame

Year released: 1963

Description: Five couples attempt to avoid pregnancy by using contraceptive pills

Infidelity in Suburbia

Cast: Sarah Butler, Marcus Rosner, Peter Benson, Arlo Hajdu

Director: David Winning

Year released: 2017

Description: A tale about infidelity, as the title explains.

By Appointment Only

Cast: Ally Walker

Director: John Terlesky

Year released: 2007

Description: A mysterious man enters the life of a real estate agent and her son.

A Frosty Affair

Cast: Jewel Staite, Shawn Roberts, Cindy Busby
  Director: Dylan Pearce
  Year released: 2015
  Description: A teacher, travelling to the city for her marriage, is forced by circumstances to travel with a stranger. What happens next?

Pocketful of Miracles

Cast: Bette Davis and Glenn Ford
    Director: Frank Capra
    Year released: 1961
    Description: Glenn Ford, Bette Davis and Frank Capra.
I'd give this Film 7 stars if I could.

Sunday in New York

Cast: Jane Fonda, Rod Taylor and Cliff Robertson.
Director: Peter Tewksbury
Year released: 1963
Description: This is a romantic comedy with several twists and turns.

Revenge of the Bridesmaids

Cast: Raven-Symoné and Joanna García
   Director: James Hayman
   Year released: 2010
   Description: How two bridesmaids foil a sham wedding to reunite old lovers

A Strange Affair

Cast: Judith Light and Jay Thomas.

Director: Ted Kotcheff

Year released: 1996

Description: A love triangle need not go one way or the other.

The Fixer

Cast: Jon Voight, Brenda Bakke, J.J. Johnston
   Director: Charles Robert Carner
   Year released: 1998
   Description: A lawyer with no scruples of conscience is finally forced to face some hard truths

Flight

Cast: Denzel Washington
  Director: Robert Zemeckis
  Year released: 2012
  Description: An airline pilot crashlands his plane. Everyone survives but it is later revealed that he was flying under the influence of alcohol and cocaine.

Mr Deeds goes to town

Cast: Gary Cooper and Jean Arthur
Director: Frank Capra
Year released: 1936
Description: A small town poet inherits 20 million dollars from his uncle. For obvious reasons, drama follows.

Underground

Cast: Jeffrey Lynn and Philip Dorn

Director: Vincent Sherman

Year released: 1941

Description: Two brothers on opposite sides of the political spectrum. One, a Nazi and the other, part of the German Nazi resistance.

Fools Parade

Cast: James Stewart and George Kennedy
   Director: Andrew V. McLaglen
   Year released: 1971
   Description: Sometimes criminals and lawkeepers play opposing roles.

The Ratings Game

Cast: Danny DeVito, Rhea Perlman
    Director: Danny DeVito
    Year released: 1984
    Description:
    This is a comedy film that will make you cry. The title gives you an idea of the subject - TV Ratings.

Boychoir

(also known as 'Hear my Song')

Cast: Dustin Hoffman, Kathy Bates, Debra Winger, Josh Lucas

Director: François Girard

Year released: 2015

Description: What happens to an illegitimate child

Never been kissed

Cast: Drew Barrymore, Jessica Alba, David Arquette, Michael Vartan.

Director: Raja Gosnell

Year released: 1999

Description: A beautiful, simple girl getting on in years finally finds love.

The Fifth Mind

Cast: Julia Duvall, Jack Diamond, Victoria Gilson
  Director: Naoko Tajima
  Year released: 2007
  Description: Two siblings with a shared traumatic childhood experience find different ways to deal with it.

Soldier Boy

Cast: Andrey Andreev, Darya Ursulyak, Viktor Dobronravov

Director: Viktoria Fanasiutina

Year released: 2019

Description: A young boy loses his parents to war and is adopted by a German regiment. A true story.

Murder by Contract

Cast: Vince Edwards
Director: Irving Lerner
Year released: 1958
Description: Martin Scorsese, cited Murder by Contract as "the film that has influenced [him] most." (Wikipedia)

The Big Combo

Cast: Cornel Wilde, Richard Conte and Brian Donlev
Director: Joseph H. Lewis
Year released: 1955
Description: A cop and criminal story

The Bravados

Cast: Gregory Peck and Joan Collins
Director: Henry King
Year released: 1958
Description: A western. A rancher pursues 4 outlaws he thought killed his wife.

Winter of Frozen Dreams

Cast: Thora Birch, Keith Carradine, and Brendan Sexton II
Director: Eric Mandelbaum
Year released: 2009
Description: A detective pursues a complex female killer.

I'll be seeing you

Cast: Alison Eastwood, Iris Quinn, Bo Swenson
  Director: Will Dixon
  Year released: 2004
  Description: A young woman discovers truths about her father.

Good Day for it

Cast: Robert Patrick, Samantha Mathis, Lance Henriksen
Director: Nick Stagliano
Year released: 2011
Description: Family, crime and revenge

Istanbul

Cast: Errol Flynn, Cornell Borchers
   Director: Joseph Pevney
   Year released: 1957
   Description: Decidedly a thriller with a liberal dose of romance

The Walking Target

Cast: Joan Evans, Merry Anders, and Ronald Foster.
   Director: Edward L. Cahn
   Year released: 1960
   Description: The story follows an ex-convict.

The Inspectors

Cast: Louis Gossett Jr., Jonathan Silverman, Tobias Mehler
Director: Brad Turner
Year released: 1998
Description: The Inspectors here are not cops, but Postal Inspectors, and who says there's any less thrill in the lives of Postal Inspectors.

Broken Trust

Cast: Tom Selleck, Elizabeth McGovern, William Atherton
Director: Geoffrey Sax
Year released: 1995
Description: Corruption in the courtroom

CHAPTER FIFTY-TWO

Patterns

Cast: Van Heflin, Everett Sloane, Ed Begley
   Director: Fielder Cook
   Year released: 1956
   Description: Niceness vs Toughness in a corporate context

Behind the Mask

Cast: Donald Sutherland, Mathew Fox, Mary McDonnell
  Director: Tom McLoughlin
  Year released: 1999
  Description: A relationship story.

Steel Toes

Cast: David Strathairn

Director: David Gow, Mark Adam

Year released: 2007

Description: A lawyer faces the toughest challenge of his life.

What's Eating Gilbert Grape

Cast: Johnny Depp, Leonardo DiCaprio, Juliette Lewis and Darlene Cates

Director: Lasse Hallström

Year released: 1993

Description: Shot when Leonardo Dicaprio was barely 19. You'll discover why he is such a phenomenal talent.

Night Alarm

Cast: Bruce Cabot

Director: Spencer Gordon Bennet

Year released: 1934

Description: A reporter seeks some excitement.

A Strange Adventure

Cast: Joan Evans, Ben Cooper, Marla English, Jan Merlin, Nick Adams, Peter Miller.
Director: William Witney
Year released: 1956
Description: A thriller, a 3-ller, actually.

Half a sinner

Cast: Heather Angel
    Director: Al Christie
    Year released: 1940
    Description: A young schoolteacher seeks adventure.

Undercover Agent

Cast: Russell Gleason, Shirley Deane, and J. M. Kerrigan
Director: Howard Bretherton
Year released: 1939
Description: The undercover agent is a railway postal clerk

Heat

Cast: Al Pacino, Robert De Niro, Tom Sizemore, Jon Voight, Val Kilmer
Director: Michael Mann
Year released: 1 995
Description: Cops and criminals and relationships

They made me a fugitive

Cast: Trevor Howard, Sally Gray
   Director: Alberto Cavalcanti
   Year released: 1947
   Description: A law-abiding citizen falls into the grip of crime, as the title indicates.

CHAPTER SIXTY-TWO

Kiss and Tell

Cast: Cheryl Ladd, John Terry, Francie Swift
   Director: Andy Wolk
   Year released: 1996
   Description: A wife's dream life is disturbed by her husband's probable mistress.

So Goes my Love

Cast: Myrna Loy, Don Ameche
    Director: Frank Ryan
    Year released: 1946
    Description: A relationship film with humour. Based on a true story.

Blue, White and Perfect

Cast: Lloyd Nolan, Mary Beth Hughes, and Helene Reynolds

Director: Herbert I. Leeds

Year released: 1942

Description: An American private detective mystery film

CHAPTER SIXTY-FIVE

Somewhere in the night

Cast: John Hodiak, Nancy Guild

Director: Joseph L. Mankiewicz

Year released: 1946

Description: An amnesiac American soldier returns from World War II badly injured. He tries to find his old identity and stumbles on a murder mystery.

The Contract

Cast: Morgan Freeman, John Cusack

Director: Bruce Beresford

Year released: 2006

Description: The paths of a contract killer and an ordinary schoolteacher cross.

Exemplary Officer

Korean Film

Description:

A man is accused by his wife of being 'a very boring person' and that very day turns out to be the most exciting day in his life.

For all time

Cast: Mark Harmon, Mary McDonnell, and Catherine Hicks
Director: Steven Schachter
Year released: 2000
Description: A beautiful story around time travel

CHAPTER SIXTY-NINE

Across the bridge

Cast: Rod Steiger, Bernard Lee

Director: Ken Annakin

Year released: 1957

Description: This Film will surprise you and could make you cry

The Take

Cast: Billy Dee Williams, Eddie Albert, Frankie Avalon, Sorrell Booke, Tracy Reed, and Albert Salmi.

Director: Robert Hartford-Davis

Year released: 1974

Description: As the title suggests, this is the story of a cop 'on the take'.

It's a wonderful world

Cast: Claudette Colbert and James Stewart
Director: W. S. Van Dyke
Year released: 1939
Description: Suspense, action, thrill, romance, comedy, the film inhabits a wonderful world.

State of the Union

Cast: Spencer Tracy, Katharine Hepburn, Van Johnson

Director: Frank Capra
Year released: 2005
Description: Drama around a man running for President. Wit of the highest order.

A farewell to arms

Cast: Rock Hudson, Jennifer Jones, Vittorio De Sica
Director: Charles Vidor, John Huston
Year released: 1957
Description: Romance in the backdrop of World War I

Behind Green Lights

Cast: Carole Landis, William Gargan, Don Beddoe
Director: Otto Brower
Year released: 1946
Description: A story with cops, criminals, journalists and politicians

Account Rendered

Cast: Griffith Jones, Ursula Howells, Honor Blackman
Director: Peter Graham Scott
Year released: 1957
Description: A crime film

Fear No More

Cast: Mala Powers, Jacques Bergerac and Anna Lee Carroll.
   Director: Bernard Wiesen
   Year released: 1961
   Description: A woman becomes a murder suspect.

Escape in the fog

Cast: Otto Kruger, Nina Foch, William Wright
    Director: Budd Boetticher
    Year released: 1945
    Description: A woman's premonition in the backdrop of war, spies and crime.

Tokyo File 212

Cast: Florence Marly, Robert Peyton, Tetsu Nakamura
   Director: Dorrell McGowan, Stuart E. McGowan
   Year released: 1951
   Description: A Japanese-American co-production of a spy film.

Identity Unknown

Cast: Richard Arlen, Cheryl Walker, Roger Pryor
   Director: Walter Colmes
   Year released: 1945
   Description: Near the end of World War II, an amnesiac soldier must find his true identity.

Point Last Seen

Cast: Linda Hamilton, Kevin Kilner, Sam Hennings
    Director: Elodie Keene
    Year released: 1998
    Description: A tracker searches for a little girl in the
desert, and confronts the pain of her own loss.

Cause for Alarm

Cast: Loretta Young, Barry Sullivan, Bruce Cowling
Director: Tay Garnett
Year released: 1951
Description: A suspense film revolving around a letter

CHAPTER EIGHTY-TWO

Never Let go

Cast: Richard Todd, Peter Sellers, Elizabeth Sellars
   Director: John Guillermin
   Year released: 1960
   Description: A petty car thief steals a particular car and drama unfolds

Jack and Sarah

Cast: Richard E. Grant, Samantha Mathis, Judi Dench, Eileen Atkins, Cherie Lunghi, Ian McKellen
Director: Tim Sullivan
Year released: 1995
Description: Fathers and daughters. And daughters and fathers.

The Outsider

Cast: Tim Daly and Naomi Watts
Director: Randa Haines
Year released: 2002
Description: A western with romance.

The Girl in the Cafe

Cast: Bill Nighy, Kelly Macdonald, Marit Velle Kile
   Director: David Yates
   Year released: 2005
   Description: What happens when a top bureaucrat asks
a simply girl to accompany him to a high-profile event.

That Uncertain feeling

Cast: Merle Oberon, Melvyn Douglas, Burgess Meredith
 Director: Ernst Lubitsch
 Year released: 1941
 Description: A lovely comedy with romance.

Guest in the House

Cast: Anne Baxter, Ralph Bellamy
Director: John Brahm
Year released: 1944
Description: A cranky, conspiring woman throws a family into disarray.

The Third Visitor

Cast: Sonia Dresdel, Guy Middleton, Karel Stepanek
Director: Maurice Elvey
Year released: 1951
Description: Have you seen a thriller where the suspense is maintained almost till the last frame?

The House of Mystery

Cast: Ed Lowry, Verna Hillie, John Sheehan
   Director: William Nigh
   Year released: 1934
   Description: An ancient curse and a killer ape

The Ghost Train

Cast: : Arthur Askey; Richard Murdoch

Director: Walter Forde

Year released: 1941

Description: Some train passengers are stranded in the night and drama follows.

I killed that man

Cast: Ricardo Cortez, Ralf Harolde
Director: Phil Rosen
Year released: 1941
Description: How the mastermind is revealed.

Emergency Wedding

Cast: Larry Parks, Barbara Hale.
Director: Edward Buzzell
Year released: 1950
Description: How a rich brat comes to his senses.

In the French Style

Cast: Jean Seberg, Stanley Baker, Philippe Forquet
Director: Robert Parrish
Year released: 1963
Description: A young girl's discovery of life in the backdrop of art.

Phone call from a stranger

Cast: Gary Merrill, Bette Davis, Shelley Winters, Michael Rennie, Keenan Wynn

Director: Jean Negulesco

Year released: 1952

Description: When you reach about 60% of the Film, you will learn why this is such an apt title for this Film.

The Lineup

Cast: Eli Wallach, Robert Keith, Warner Anderson
Director: Don Siegel
Year released: 1958
Description: Two cops and drugdealers.

The Trollenberg terror

Cast: Forrest Tucker, Laurence Payne, Jennifer Jayne, Janet Munro.

Director: Quentin Lawrence

Year released: 1958

Description: An early special effects Film with extra-terrrestrials.

Deadly whispers

Cast: Tony Danza, Pamela Reed
Director: Bill L. Norton
Year released: 1995
Description: A man's mental disorder is the centrepiece of this murder mystery.

A closed book

Cast: Daryl Hannah, Jane Ryder, Tom Conti
    Director: Raúl Ruiz
    Year released: 2010
    Description: A blind author and his secretary promise riveting drama.

Against a crooked sky

Cast: Richard Boone, Stewart Petersen, Henry Wilcoxon.
Director: Earl Bellamy
Year released: 1975
Description: This is a western with a relatively larger landscape, literally and figuratively.

A lady takes a chance

Cast: Jean Arthur, John Wayne
    Director: William A. Seiter
    Year released: 1943
    Description: Three guys are behind a girl when she meets a fourth.

* 9 7 9 8 8 8 8 6 4 1 1 7 2 0 *